THE SEVEN GREATEST
WORDS OF LOVE

THE SEVEN GREATEST WORDS OF LOVE
A Seven-Session Video-Based Study for Small Groups or Individuals

Published by Purpose Driven Publishers
23182 Arroyo Vista
Rancho Santa Margarite, CA 92688

ISBN: 978-1-4228-0432-2

Printed and bound in the United States of America.

TABLE OF CONTENTS

HOW TO USE THIS
VIDEO CURRICULUM

Here is a brief explanation of the features of this study guide.

CHECKING IN:

You will open each meeting with an opportunity for everyone to check in with each other about how you are doing with the weekly assignments. Accountability is a key to success in this study!

KEY VERSE:

Each week you will find a key verse or Scripture passage for your group to read together. If someone in the group has a different translation, ask them to read it aloud so the group can get a bigger picture of the meaning of the passage.

VIDEO LESSON:

There is a video lesson for the group to watch together each week. Fill in the blanks in the lesson outlines as you watch the video, and be sure to refer back to these outlines during your discussion time.

DISCOVERY QUESTIONS:

Each video segment is complemented by several questions for group discussion. Please don't feel pressured to discuss every single question. There is no reason to rush through the answers. Give everyone ample opportunity to share their thoughts. If you don't get through all of the discussion questions, that's okay.

PUTTING IT INTO PRACTICE:

This is where the rubber meets the road. We don't want to be just hearers of the Word. We also need to be doers of the Word (James 1:22). These assignments are application exercises that will help you put into practice the truths you have discussed in the lesson.

PRAYER DIRECTION:

At the end of each session you will find suggestions for your group prayer time. Praying together is one of the greatest privileges of small group life. Please don't take it for granted.

A TIP FOR THE HOST

The study guide material is meant to be your servant, not your master. The point is not to race through the sessions; the point is to take time to let God work in your lives. Nor is it necessary to "go around the circle" before you move on to the next question. Give people the freedom to speak, but don't insist on it. Your group will enjoy deeper, more open sharing and discussion if people don't feel pressured to speak up.

SESSION 1:
The Word of Forgiveness

If this is your first time meeting as a group, or if you have any new group members, take a few minutes to introduce yourselves.

This week Pastor Rick teaches *The Word of Forgiveness* from Jesus when he was on the cross. Because of what Jesus did, we can experience God's grace and have a relationship with him.

KEY VERSE:

"Jesus said, 'Father, forgive them,
for they do not know what they are doing.'"
LUKE 23:34 (NIV)

Great crowds trailed along behind, and many grief-stricken women.
But Jesus turned and said to them, "Daughters of Jerusalem, don't weep
for me, but for yourselves"... Two others, criminals, were led out to be
executed with him at a place called "The Skull." There all three were
crucified—Jesus on the center cross, and the two criminals on either side.

LUKE 23:27-28, 32-33 (TLB)

Jesus said, "Father, forgive them, for they don't know what they are
doing." And the soldiers gambled for his clothes by throwing dice. The
crowd watched and the leaders scoffed. "He saved others," they said,
"let him save himself if he is really God's Messiah, the Chosen One."
The soldiers mocked him, too, by offering him a drink of sour wine.
They called out to him, "If you are the King of the Jews, save yourself!"

LUKE 23:34-37 (NLT)

1.) We _____ it.

> *"When I refused to confess my sin, my body wasted away, and I groaned all day long . . . My strength evaporated like water in the summer heat. Finally, I confessed all my sins to you and stopped trying to hide my guilt. I said to myself, "I will confess my rebellion to the LORD." And you forgave me! All my guilt is gone."*
>
> **PSALM 32:3-5 (NLT)**

HOW WE BURY THE PAST

- _____
- _____
- _____

> *"You will never succeed in life if you try to hide your sins."*
>
> **PROVERBS 28:13 (GNT)**

2.) We _____ others.

> *"Yes," Adam admitted, "but it was the woman you gave me who brought me some, and I ate it."*
>
> **GENESIS 3:12 (TLB)**

> *"People's own foolishness ruins their lives, but in their minds they blame the Lord."*
>
> **PROVERBS 19:3 (NCV)**

3.) We _____ ourselves up.

> *"My guilt has overwhelmed me like a burden too heavy to bear. I am bowed down and brought very low; all day long I go about mourning."*
>
> **PSALM 38:4, 6 (NIV)**

1.) _____ it.

> *"The LORD gave us mind and conscience;*
> *we cannot hide from ourselves."*
> **PROVERBS 20:27 (GNT)**

> *"If we claim to be without sin, we deceive ourselves*
> *and the truth is not in us."*
> **1 JOHN 1:8 (NIV)**

TO STOP _____ MYSELF, I MUST

STOP _____ MYSELF.

2.) _____ responsibility.

> *"I recognize my faults; I am always conscious of my sins."*
> **PSALM 51:3 (GNT)**

> *"Admit your faults to one another and pray for each other*
> *so that you may be healed."*
> **JAMES 5:16 (TLB)**

I'M ONLY AS SICK AS MY SECRETS.

3.) _____ for forgiveness.

> *"If we freely admit that we have sinned, we find God utterly reliable . . .*
> *he forgives our sins and makes us thoroughly clean from all that is evil."*
> **1 JOHN 1:9 (PHILLIPS)**

GOD IS MORE WILLING TO FORGIVE YOU THAN YOU ARE WILLING TO ADMIT YOUR SIN.

"Yes, all have sinned . . . yet now God declares us "not guilty" . . . if we trust in Jesus Christ, who in his kindness freely takes away our sins."

ROMANS 3:23-24 (TLB)

WHAT GOD DOES WITH MY GUILT

1.) God forgives _____.

2.) God forgives _____.

"He has forgiven you all your sins: Christ has utterly wiped out the damning evidence of broken laws and commandments which always hung over our heads, and has completely annulled it by nailing it over his own head on the cross."

COLOSSIANS 2:13-14 (PHILLIPS)

3.) God forgives _____.

"For he [Christ] is always living to intercede on their behalf."

HEBREWS 7:25 (PHILLIPS)

4.) God forgives _____.

GOD WANTS YOU TO NEVER FORGET WHAT IT COST JESUS TO PAY FOR YOUR SINS.

"What happiness for those whose guilt has been forgiven! . . . What relief for those who . . . God has cleared their record."

PSALM 32:1-2 (TLB)

1.) The three most common ways we deal with guilt are by burying it, blaming others, or beating ourselves up. How do you typically deal with guilt, and how has it affected your relationships? You don't have to answer this publicly, but are you holding on to any guilt? What does this lesson say you should do?

2.) Pastor Rick teaches that Jesus wants us to admit our guilt, accept responsibility for our actions, and ask for forgiveness. Why is it important to admit our guilt rather than just assume everything is okay with God? Why is it important to take responsibility for our actions? What does "taking responsibility" look like?

3.) God forgives us freely, but if we want to be set free from our guilt we have to confess our faults to each other. Why do you think it is important to confess your sins to one other person? Do you know someone you trust enough to confess your sins to? If not, what's keeping you from having a relationship like that? Are you the kind of person that someone can trust if they confess their sins to you?

Take time this week to ask God to reveal anything in your life that needs to be confessed. Keep in mind that God is for you, and not against you (check out Romans 8:31). He's not surprised by your confession, and he will forgive you instantly, completely, repeatedly, and freely.

Write down anything the Holy Spirit brings to mind. You don't have to show anyone this list—it can just be for you. Pray over your list, and as you confess each sin, go through these steps: Admit your sin, accept responsibility for it, and ask for forgiveness.

PRAYER DIRECTION:

As you pray, thank God that he forgives you instantly, completely, repeatedly, and freely. This week, ask him to show you specifically what that means and help you to believe that truth in the depths of your heart. Tell God you want him to show you any hidden sins in your life, and trust the Holy Spirit to reveal them.

Then, admit your guilt, accept responsibility for what you did (or didn't do), and ask God to forgive you. Ask him to help you *fully* accept his forgiveness and to show you that you are beloved and accepted in his family.

SESSION 2:

The Word of Assurance

CHECKING IN:

Last week we learned that *The Word of Forgiveness* from Jesus means we can experience God's grace, which allows us to have a relationship with God. What has God shown you about forgiveness during this past week? This week we're going to learn how Jesus told us from the cross that we can be certain of our salvation.

KEY VERSE:

"And Jesus replied, 'I assure you,
today you will be with me in paradise.'"
LUKE 23:43 (NLT)

One of the criminals hanging beside him scoffed, "So you're the Messiah, are you? Prove it by saving yourself—and us, too, while you're at it!" But the other criminal protested, "Don't you fear God even when you have been sentenced to die? We deserve to die for our crimes, but this man hasn't done anything wrong." Then he said, "Jesus, remember me when you come into your Kingdom." And Jesus replied, "I assure you, today you will be with me in paradise."

LUKE 23:39-43 (NLT)

(5 Truths That Saved the Dying Thief)

1.) I must know _____ after I die.

> *"Everyone must die once, and after that be judged by God."*
> **HEBREWS 9:27 (GNT)**

2.) I must know that I've _____.

> *"We deserve to die for our evil deeds."*
> **LUKE 23:41 (TLB)**

> *"If we confess our sins, he is faithful and just and will forgive us our sins and purify us from all unrighteousness."*
> **1 JOHN 1:9 (NIV)**

> *"For the wages of sin is death, but the gift of God is eternal life in Christ Jesus our Lord."*
> **ROMANS 6:23 (NIV)**

3.) I must know that Jesus was _____.

> *"But this man has done nothing wrong."*
> **LUKE 23:41 (NIV)**

> *"Not a single person on earth is always good and never sins."*
> **ECCLESIASTES 7:20 (NLT)**

> *"God had Christ, who was sinless, take our sin so that we might receive God's approval through him."*
> **2 CORINTHIANS 5:21 (GW)**

4.) I must know that only _____ can save me.

"Then he said, 'Jesus, remember me.'"
LUKE 23:42 (NIV)

*"For it is by grace you have been saved, through faith—and this not
from yourselves, it is the gift of God—not by works,
so that no one can boast."*
EPHESIANS 2:8-9 (NIV)

5.) I must know Jesus will save me _____.

"Jesus, remember me when you come into your kingdom."
LUKE 23:42 (NIV)

"Believe in the Lord Jesus, and you will be saved."
ACTS 16:31 (NIV)

On the _____ of God's Word

"And Jesus replied, 'I assure you, today you will be with me in paradise.'"

LUKE 23:43 (NLT)

SALVATION IS. . .

- _____ *("Today")*
- _____ *("you will")*
- _____ *("be with me")*
- _____ *("in paradise")*

"This is the hour to receive God's favor; today is the day to be saved!"

2 CORINTHIANS 6:2 (GNT)

"For 'Everyone who calls on the name of the LORD will be saved.'"

ROMANS 10:13 (NLT)

1.) Have you ever been unsure about your salvation? If so, what have you learned in this lesson that will help you overcome that uncertainty?

2.) If you struggle with uncertainty about your salvation, let's take care of that right now. Tell God that you have accepted the gift of salvation, that you receive his grace in faith, and that you want to reaffirm your trust and belief in Jesus as your Savior. Now, sign and date below when you have done this. Next time Satan starts telling you that you really aren't a believer, and tries to plant seeds of doubt, remember this covenant, and thank God for your salvation.

Pastor Rick teaches that when we pray to receive salvation, the words we use don't matter; it's all about the condition of your heart. What do you think about that? What are the essential elements of any prayer of salvation?

3.) How does knowing a salvation prayer doesn't have to be perfectly worded help you overcome the fear of sharing Christ with others?

This week memorize the following verse: *"Jesus answered him, 'Truly I tell you, today you will be with me in paradise'"* (Luke 23:43 NIV). Each day thank God that your salvation is immediate (*"Today"*), certain (*"you will"*), that it is based on a relationship with Jesus (*"be with me"*), and that it is forever (*"in paradise"*).

PRAYER DIRECTION:

As you pray together with your group, begin by thanking God for his promise of salvation. Pray that God will develop your faith more and more each day. Then ask him to help you live anchored in the fact that you're saved by grace and not by works. Finally, pray for those who still need to hear the Good News of Christ.

SESSION 3:

The Word of Love

Last week we talked about spending time in thankful prayer because Jesus told us from the cross that we could be certain of our salvation. How did an attitude of gratitude impact your week? What kind of new experiences did you have? How did people respond?

KEY VERSE:

"When Jesus saw his mother standing there beside the disciple he loved, he said to her, 'Dear woman, here is your son.' And he said to this disciple, 'Here is your mother.'"

JOHN 19:26-27 (NLT)

Near the cross of Jesus stood his mother, his mother's sister, Mary the wife of Clopas, and Mary Magdalene. When Jesus saw his mother there, and the disciple whom he loved standing nearby, he said to her, "Woman, here is your son," and to the disciple, "Here is your mother." From that time on, this disciple took her into his home.

JOHN 19:25-27 (NIV)

1.) Care for my _____.

Love isn't just something you say, it's something you do.

We show the love of Jesus to our family

- By _____

- By meeting _____

> *"Show respect for widows who really are all alone. But if a widow has*
> *children or grandchildren, they should learn first to carry out their*
> *religious duties toward their own family and in this way repay their*
> *parents and grandparents, because that is what pleases God."*
> **1 TIMOTHY 5:3-4 (GNT)**

> *"Anyone who does not provide for their relatives,*
> *and especially for their own household,*
> *has denied the faith and is worse than an unbeliever."*
> **1 TIMOTHY 5:8 (NIV)**

- By giving _____

> *"Friends love through all kinds of weather,*
> *and families stick together in all kinds of trouble."*
> **PROVERBS 17:17 (THE MESSAGE)**

2.) Treat _____ as my family.

> *"For whoever does the will of my Father in heaven*
> *is my brother and sister and mother."*
> **MATTHEW 12:50 (NIV)**

"Do not rebuke an older man, but appeal to him as if he were your father. Treat the younger men as your brothers, the older women as mothers, and the younger women as sisters, with all purity."
1 TIMOTHY 5:1-2 (GNT)

"Be devoted to each other like a loving family. Excel in showing respect for each other."
ROMANS 12:10 (GW)

"When we have the opportunity to help anyone, we should do it. But we should give special attention to those who are in the family of believers."
GALATIANS 6:10 (NCV)

"Share each other's burdens, and in this way obey the law of Christ."
GALATIANS 6:2 (NLT)

3.) Learn to see _____ even when I'm in pain.

"You must have the same attitude that Christ Jesus had."
PHILIPPIANS 2:5 (NLT)

"Since Christ suffered and underwent pain, you must have the same attitude he did; you must be ready to suffer, too. For remember, when your body suffers, sin loses its power."
1 PETER 4:1 (TLB)

4.) Meet _____ even if mine aren't met.

"Each one of us needs to look after the good of the people around us,
asking ourselves, 'How can I help?'"
ROMANS 15:2 (THE MESSAGE)

Look for Jesus disguised as a _____

"When God's people are in need, be ready to help them.
Always be eager to practice hospitality."
ROMANS 12:13 (NLT)

WHEN GRIEVING . . .

- _____ that Jesus cares about your pain.
- _____ love from others.
- _____ somebody else to help.

1.) One of the ways we love like Jesus is to care for our own family. Is there anything you need to change in the way you show love to the members of your family?

2.) What do you think about the idea that you should look for Jesus disguised as a hurting person? How might that change the way you think and act toward them?

3.) The Bible says we should treat other believers like our family. Talk about why that is important. Include John 13:35 in your conversation: *"Your love for one another will prove to the world that you are my disciples"* (NLT).

4.) What are some of the reasons you think God encourages us to use our pain to comfort others? How have you been comforted by someone else who went through a similar experience? In what ways can you help others based on some of the difficult things you have experienced in your life?

5.) To love like Jesus is to meet others' needs even when your needs aren't being met. What is one thing you can start doing today that will help you love this way?

PUTTING IT INTO PRACTICE:

One of the best expressions of love is time. The most valuable thing you can give someone is your attention, because when you give attention to somebody you're saying, "You matter to me. You are valuable. You are worth listening to. You are worth my time."

- **What are some of the ways you can offer love to your family and friends this week through giving your time?**

- **What are some practical ways to love and care for the other believers in your community and treat them as if they were a part of your family?**

- **What changes do you need to make in your schedule so that you have more time to demonstrate your love through action?**

PRAYER DIRECTION:

Dear Jesus, I want to be more loving. I want to work on my relationships. I want to learn to love you with all of my heart. And I want to learn to love everybody else. I want to be known as the most loving person people know. So I'm going to make it my primary value in life, my number one goal to learn to love you and to learn to love other people because it's all about love. Lord, I've got a lot of hurts in my heart that need to be healed. I need to be filled with your love. I can't give to others what I don't feel. I need to feel forgiven. I need to experience your grace. I need to know your love so it can overflow out of my life into others. Replace my fears with your love. Replace my hurts with your peace. I want to learn to know you and love you, Jesus Christ, and I want to be a loving person. In your name I pray. Amen."

SESSION 4:

The Word of Substitution

CHECKING IN:

Last week we talked about putting the needs of others ahead of our own. How did you put that into action? What did God show you through your faithfulness? How did putting the needs of others ahead of your own stretch your faith?

This week Pastor Rick teaches how God nailed our sins to the cross, with Jesus allowing us to connect with God through the holiness of Jesus.

KEY VERSE:

"At noon, darkness fell across the whole land until three o'clock.
At about three o'clock, Jesus called out with a loud voice,
'Eli, Eli, lema sabachthani?' which means, 'My God, my God,
why have you abandoned me?'"
MATTHEW 27:45-46 (NLT)

Jesus became my _____

> *"He is the atoning sacrifice for our sins, and not only for ours
> but also for the sins of the whole world."*
> **1 JOHN 2:2 (NIV)**

ATONEMENT = PAYMENT FOR DAMAGE DONE

> *"God took the sinless Christ and poured into him our sins.
> Then, in exchange, he poured God's goodness into us!"*
> **2 CORINTHIANS 5:21 (TLB)**

WHAT DOES IT TEACH US?

1.) God is _____!

> *"Holy, holy, holy is the Lord God Almighty,
> who was, and is, and is to come."*
> **REVELATION 4:8 (NIV)**

> *"Your eyes are too pure to look on evil;
> you cannot tolerate wrongdoing."*
> **HABAKKUK 1:13 (NIV)**

2.) Sin is _____!

- Sin _____ me from God

> *"It is your evil that has separated you from your God.*
> *Your sins cause him to turn away from you, so he does not hear you."*
> **ISAIAH 59:2 (NCV)**

- Sin _____ me

> *"My guilt has overwhelmed me like a burden too heavy to bear."*
> **PSALM 38:4 (NIV)**

- Sin _____ me

> *"God is a righteous judge and always condemns the wicked."*
> **PSALM 7:11 (GNT)**

RIGHTEOUS = GOD ALWAYS DOES WHAT'S RIGHT

> *"For the wages of sin is death, but the gift of God*
> *is eternal life in Christ Jesus our Lord."*
> **ROMANS 6:23 (NIV)**

3.) Salvation is _____.

> *"For God sent Christ Jesus to take the punishment for our sins and to*
> *end all God's anger against us. He used Christ's blood and our faith as*
> *the means of saving us from his wrath."*
> **ROMANS 3:25 (TLB)**

> *"But Christ has rescued us from the curse pronounced by the law.*
> *When he was hung on the cross, he took upon himself*
> *the curse for our wrongdoing."*
> **GALATIANS 3:13 (NLT)**

WHAT SHOULD BE MY RESPONSE?

1.) _____ from my sin and _____ Jesus to save me.

> *"We are made right with God by placing our faith in Jesus Christ.*
> *And this is true for everyone who believes, no matter who we are."*
> **ROMANS 3:22 (NLT)**

> *"If we deliberately keep on sinning after we have received the*
> *knowledge of the truth, no sacrifice for sins is left."*
> **HEBREWS 10:26 (NIV)**

2.) Live in a state of _____.

> *"So now we can rejoice in our wonderful new relationship with God*
> *because our Lord Jesus Christ has made us friends of God."*
> **ROMANS 5:11 (NLT)**

3.) When I'm tempted, _____ what my sin cost Jesus.

> *"For you know that God paid a ransom to save you from the empty life you inherited from your ancestors. And it was not paid with mere gold or silver . . . It was the precious blood of Christ, the sinless, spotless Lamb of God."*
> **1 PETER 1:18-19 (NLT)**

4.) Tell others _____!

> *"[God] is patient for your sake. He doesn't want to destroy anyone but wants all people to have an opportunity to turn to him and change the way they think and act."*
> **2 PETER 3:9 (GW)**

DISCOVERY QUESTIONS:

1.) Pastor Rick teaches that when we are tempted, we should remember what our sin cost Jesus. How would that help you overcome temptation?

2.) How would your life look different if you were to live with more gratitude toward Jesus on a daily basis? What are ways you can show your gratitude to Jesus?

One of the ways you can tell others about your faith in Jesus is to tell them about the things God has taught you. Take some time this week to answer these questions. This will help you think of ways to share with others how God is working in your life.

- **What has God taught me from failure? (Psalm 51)**
- **What has God taught me from a lack of money? (Philippians 4:11-13)**
- **What has God taught me from pain or sorrow or depression? (2 Corinthians 1:4-10)**
- **What has God taught me through waiting? (Psalm 40)**
- **What has God taught me through illness? (Psalm 119:71)**
- **What has God taught me from disappointment? (Genesis 50:20)**

PRAYER DIRECTION:

As you begin your prayer time, start by thanking Jesus for what he did for you on the cross. Ask him to help you live in a continual posture of gratitude. Let God know you want to share the Good News with others. Pray this simple but powerful two-word prayer: "Use me."

SESSION 5:

The Word of Humanity

Last week we learned that Jesus paid for our sins by dying on the cross, allowing us to connect to God through the holiness of Jesus. Did anything happen this week that reminded you why we need a Savior to break us free from our sins? Share your experiences with the group.

This week we'll see that the humanity of Jesus is a reminder that we should serve those in need, and that God will use our suffering to help others.

KEY VERSE:

"After this, Jesus knew that everything had been done. So that the Scripture would come true, he said, 'I am thirsty.'"
JOHN 19:28 (NCV)

After this, Jesus knew that everything had been done. So that the Scripture would come true, he said, "I am thirsty." There was a jar full of vinegar there, so the soldiers soaked a sponge in it, put the sponge on a branch of a hyssop plant, and lifted it to Jesus' mouth.

JOHN 19:28-29 (NCV)

The soldiers tried to give Jesus wine mixed with myrrh to drink, but he refused.

MARK 15:23 (NCV)

1.) It showed that Jesus is _____.

"[Jesus] gave up his place with God and made himself nothing.
He was born as a man and became like a servant. And when he was
living as a man, he humbled himself and was fully obedient to God,
even when that caused his death—death on a cross."

PHILIPPIANS 2:7-8 (NCV)

2.) It showed he was the _____.

"So that Scripture would be fulfilled, Jesus said, 'I am thirsty.'"

JOHN 19:28 (NIV)

"When I was thirsty, they offered me vinegar."

PSALM 69:21 (GNT)

"Take a branch of the hyssop plant, dip it into the bowl filled with
blood, and then wipe the blood on the sides and tops of the doorframes."

EXODUS 12:22 (NCV)

3.) It shows how much Jesus _____.

"God demonstrates his own love for us in this:
While we were still sinners, Christ died for us."

ROMANS 5:8 (NIV)

"The time is surely coming," says the Sovereign LORD, "when I will send a famine on the land—not a famine of bread or water but of hearing the words of the LORD. People will stagger from sea to sea and wander from border to border searching for the word of the LORD, but they will not find it. Beautiful girls and strong young men will grow faint in that day, thirsting for the LORD'S word."

AMOS 8:11-13 (NLT)

1.) I serve Jesus by _____.

"'Lord, when did we ever see you hungry and feed you? Or thirsty and give you something to drink?' . . . And the King will say, 'I tell you the truth, when you did it to one of the least of these my brothers and sisters, you were doing it to me!'"

MATTHEW 25:37-40 (NLT)

2.) Jesus notices the _____.

"If you give even a cup of cold water to one of the least of my followers, you will surely be rewarded."

MATTHEW 10:42 (NLT)

3.) The most Christ-like service is to _____.

"If your enemies are hungry, give them food to eat. If they are thirsty, give them water to drink."

PROVERBS 25:21 (NLT)

1.) Realize what I'm _____.

"O God, you are my God, and I long for you.
My whole being desires you; like a dry, worn-out,
and waterless land, my soul is thirsty for you."
PSALM 63:1 (GNT)

"Blessed are those who hunger and thirst for righteousness,
for they will be filled."
MATTHEW 5:6 (NIV)

2.) Realize that Jesus _____.

"He took our suffering on him and felt our pain for us . . . He was
wounded for the wrong we did; he was crushed for the evil we did.
The punishment, which made us well, was given to him, and we are
healed because of his wounds."
ISAIAH 53:4-5 (NCV)

"This High Priest of ours understands our weaknesses,
for he faced all of the same testings we do, yet he did not sin."
HEBREWS 4:15 (NLT)

3.) Stop looking for _____ elsewhere.

"My people have done two evils: They have turned away from me,
the spring of living water. And they have dug their own wells,
which are broken wells that cannot hold water."
JEREMIAH 2:13 (NCV)

"On the last day, the climax of the festival, Jesus stood and shouted to the crowds, 'Anyone who is thirsty may come to me! Anyone who believes in me may come and drink! For the Scriptures declare, 'Rivers of living water will flow from his heart.'"

JOHN 7:37-38 (NLT)

"Jesus replied, 'Anyone who drinks this water will soon become thirsty again. But those who drink the water I give will never be thirsty again. It becomes a fresh, bubbling spring within them, giving them eternal life.'"

JOHN 4:13-14 (NLT)

1.) Pastor Rick says that many people go through life living outside their purpose because they trust their limited vision more than God's grand plan. God wants you to discover your purpose. What are some ways God reveals what he has planned for you?

2.) Sometimes we dig wells looking for water when Niagara Falls is flowing right behind us. How do you relate to that analogy? How did God get you to turn around and see what he wanted you to see?

3.) Jesus says real love is even serving our enemies. What do you think that means? Talk about what kind of faith that may require. What are some ways you can serve your enemies in love?

- Jesus calls us to serve like him (Matthew 20:28). He wants us to stop asking, "Who's going to meet my needs?" and start asking, "Whose needs can I meet?"

- Being a servant means you do what's needed, even when it's inconvenient. Are you available to God anytime? Can he change your plans without you becoming resentful?

- Being a servant means you do your best with what you have. What you do doesn't have to be perfect for God to use and bless it.

PRAYER DIRECTION:

As you close in prayer, focus on any areas of your life where you're feeling unfulfilled and unsatisfied. Ask God to quench that spiritual thirst.

Father, help me remember at the start of every day that I am your servant. Help me to see interruptions as divine appointments that give me an opportunity to practice serving. Help me to shift my perspective from, "Who's going to meet my needs?" to "Whose needs can I meet?" Teach me to be humble and to think of others' needs before my own. In Jesus' name I pray. Amen.

The Word of Victory

CHECKING IN:

Last week Pastor Rick taught that Jesus came as a servant, and he wants us to be servants, too. What did God reveal to you about serving this week? In what ways did God ask you to serve that surprised you or changed your perspective?

This week we'll learn why the Cross is God's conclusive statement about sin. The power of sin and death has been destroyed and the victory has already been won!

KEY VERSE:

"When he had received the drink [of wine vinegar], *Jesus said, 'It is finished.' With that, he bowed his head and gave up his spirit."*
JOHN 19:30 (NIV)

"My food," Jesus said to them, "is to obey the will of the one who sent me and to finish the work he gave me to do."

JOHN 4:34 (GNT)

Knowing that everything had now been finished, and so that Scripture would be fulfilled, Jesus said, "I am thirsty." When he had received the drink, Jesus said, "It is finished." With that, he bowed his head and gave up his spirit.

JOHN 19:28, 30 (NIV)

THE USES OF "TETELESTAI"

- Servant: *The task is completed!*
- Judge: *Justice has been served!*
- Accountant: *The debt has been paid in full!*
- Artist: *The picture is finished!*
- Priest: *The perfect offering has been given!*

WHAT DID JESUS "FINISH" ON THE CROSS?

1.) He _____ what God had promised us.

> *"He said to them, 'This is what I told you while I was still with you: Everything must be fulfilled that is written about me in the Law of Moses, the Prophets and the Psalms.' Then he opened their minds so they could understand the Scriptures. He told them, 'This is what is written: The Messiah will suffer and rise from the dead on the third day, and repentance for the forgiveness of sins will be preached in his name to all nations, beginning at Jerusalem.'"*
> **LUKE 24:44-47 (NIV)**

> *"For all of God's promises have been fulfilled in Christ with a resounding "Yes!" And through Christ, our "Amen" (which means "Yes") ascends to God for his glory."*
> **2 CORINTHIANS 1:20 (NLT)**

2.) He _____ what God's justice required.

> *"The law of Moses was unable to save us because of the weakness of our sinful nature. So God did what the law could not do. He sent his own Son in a body like the bodies we sinners have. And in that body God declared an end to sin's control over us by giving his Son as a sacrifice for our sins. He did this so that the just requirement of the law would be fully satisfied for us, who no longer follow our sinful nature but instead follow the Spirit."*
>
> **ROMANS 8:3-4 (NLT)**

> *"After [Jesus] had finished his work, he became the source of eternal salvation for everyone who obeys him."*
>
> **HEBREWS 5:9 (GW)**

> *"Here it is in a nutshell: Just as one person did it wrong and got us in all this trouble with sin and death, another person did it right and got us out of it. But more than just getting us out of trouble, he got us into life!"*
>
> **ROMANS 5:18 (THE MESSAGE)**

3.) He _____ the debt that I owed God.

> *"We owed a debt because we broke God's laws. That debt listed all the rules we failed to follow. But God forgave us that debt. He took away that debt and nailed it to the cross."*
>
> **COLOSSIANS 2:14 (ICB)**

> *"His Son paid the price to free us, which means that our sins are forgiven."*
>
> **COLOSSIANS 1:14 (GW)**

> *"And when sins have been forgiven, there is no need to offer any more sacrifices."*
>
> **HEBREWS 10:18 (NLT)**

4.) He _____ the fear of death!

"For the sin of this one man, Adam, caused death to rule over many.
But even greater is God's wonderful grace and his gift of righteousness,
for all who receive it will live in triumph over sin and death
through this one man, Jesus Christ."

ROMANS 5:17 (NLT)

"Because God's children are human beings—made of flesh and blood—
the Son also became flesh and blood. For only as a human being could
he die, and only by dying could he break the power of the devil, who
had the power of death. Only in this way could he set free all who have
lived their lives as slaves to the fear of dying."

HEBREWS 2:14-15 (NLT)

5.) He _____ Satan's power to _____ me.

"God has freed us from the power of darkness,
and brought us into the kingdom of his dear Son."

COLOSSIANS 1:13 (NCV)

"In this way God took away Satan's power to accuse you of sin,
and God openly displayed to the whole world Christ's triumph
at the cross where your sins were all taken away."

COLOSSIANS 2:15 (TLB)

"And I am certain that God, who began the good work within you,
will continue his work until it is finally finished on the day when
Christ Jesus returns."

PHILIPPIANS 1:6 (NLT)

"Saving is all his idea, and all his work. All we do is trust him enough
to let him do it. It's God's gift from start to finish!"

EPHESIANS 2:8 (THE MESSAGE)

1.) Just before Jesus died on the cross, he said, "It is finished!" What is the significance of that statement to you today? How can it transform your life? Ask God to help you move from thinking "It is finished!" is true to knowing it is true.

2.) What do you think it means when the Bible says that Jesus set us free from the fear of dying?

3.) Pastor Rick says that Christianity is the only religion where God has already done it all; we don't have to do anything. We simply trust in his grace, and our service flows from that trust. Why do you think we can struggle with feeling like we have to prove ourselves to God?

This week, memorize Ephesians 2:8-9. It is a foundational verse for understanding that victory comes from God, and not from anything we do.

> *"For it is by God's grace that you have been saved through faith.*
> *It is not the result of your own efforts, but God's gift,*
> *so that no one can boast about it."*
>
> **EPHESIANS 2:8-9 (GNT)**

There are people you know who think God will never love them because they've made such a mess of their lives. But you know God wants them to come to him as they are. Help them hear the Good News from Jesus. Invite them to come to church with you this week. It's such a simple thing to do, but it can make a difference that will last for eternity.

PRAYER DIRECTION:

As you close in prayer as a group, thank Jesus for fulfilling on the cross what God promised, for satisfying what God's justice required, for paying our debt, for defeating the fear of death, and for destroying Satan's power to control us. Praise God that the victory has already been won.

The Word of Trust

As you begin the last week of *The Seven Greatest Words of Love,* consider sharing with your small group the most important thing you've learned through this Bible study.

"Then Jesus shouted, 'Father, I entrust my spirit into your hands!'
And with those words he breathed his last."

LUKE 23:46 (NLT)

By this time it was about noon, and darkness fell across the whole land until three o'clock. The light from the sun was gone. And suddenly, the curtain in the sanctuary of the Temple was torn down the middle. Then Jesus shouted, "Father, I entrust my spirit into your hands!" And with those words he breathed his last. When the Roman officer overseeing the execution saw what had happened, he worshiped God and said, "Surely this man was innocent."

LUKE 23:44-47 (NLT)

- _____

"No one can take my life from me. I sacrifice it voluntarily. For I have the authority to lay it down when I want to and also to take it up again."
JOHN 10:18 (NLT)

- _____

- _____

Jesus focused on the _____, not his pain.

4 TRUTHS TO REMEMBER IN YOUR DARKEST HOUR

1.) I have a Father in Heaven who _____!

"I came from the Father and entered the world;
now I am leaving the world and going back to the Father."
JOHN 16:28 (NIV)

"As a father has compassion on his children,
so the LORD has compassion on those who fear him."
PSALM 103:13 (NIV)

GOD LOVES ME MORE THAN I DO.

2.) My Father can be _____!

> *"For the word of the LORD holds true,*
> *and we can trust everything he does."*
> **PSALM 33:4 (NLT)**

> *"I am suffering here in prison. But I am not ashamed of it,*
> *for I know the one in whom I trust, and I am sure that he is able to*
> *guard what I have entrusted to him until the day of his return."*
> **2 TIMOTHY 1:12 (NLT)**

3.) My Father is taking care of things _____!

WHILE YOU'RE WAITING, GOD IS WORKING.

> *"When he is at work in the north, I do not see him; when he turns to*
> *the south, I catch no glimpse of him. But he knows the way that I take;*
> *and when he has tested me, I will come forth as gold."*
> **JOB 23:9-10 (NIV)**

> *"For our light and momentary troubles are achieving for us an eternal*
> *glory that far outweighs them all. So we fix our eyes not on what is*
> *seen, but on what is unseen, since what is seen is temporary,*
> *but what is unseen is eternal."*
> **2 CORINTHIANS 4:17-18 (NIV)**

4.) My Father can handle anything I put _____.

GOD'S HANDS ARE . . .

• Big enough to _____

> *"The LORD will hold you in his hands for all to see—a splendid*
> *crown in the hand of God."*
>
> **ISAIAH 62:3 (NLT)**

• Strong enough to keep me _____

> *"I give them eternal life, and they shall never perish . . .*
> *My Father, who has given them to me, is greater than all;*
> *no one can snatch them out of my Father's hand."*
>
> **JOHN 10:28-29 (NIV)**

• Scarred with the nail prints so he _____

> *"Can a mother forget the baby at her breast and have no compassion*
> *on the child she has borne? Though she may forget, I will not forget*
> *you! See, I have engraved you on the palms of my hands."*
>
> **ISAIAH 49:15-16 (NIV)**

> *"I think you ought to know, dear brothers, about the hard time we*
> *went through in Asia. We were really crushed and overwhelmed, and*
> *feared we would never live through it. We felt we were doomed to die*
> *and saw how powerless we were to help ourselves; but that was good,*
> *for then we put everything into the hands of God, who alone could save*
> *us, for he can even raise the dead."*
>
> **2 CORINTHIANS 1:8-9 (TLB)**

1.) Why do you think it is so hard to put things into God's hands? In what ways do you struggle to trust God? What is one thing you keep trying to hold on to? Tell God you are placing it in his hands (perhaps even praying about that with the group). Then, practice this: Each time you start to take it out of God's hands, tell him you are leaving it with him. And then watch what he does!

2.) What happens to your perspective when you trust God in your darkest hour?

3.) Pastor Rick said, "While you're waiting, God is working." Share an example of when you were waiting on God but then realized later that he was working on the solution the whole time. Is there something you are waiting on now? How do your behavior and attitude line up with the FACT that God is at work, even if you can't see it yet?

PUTTING IT INTO PRACTICE:

What do you think is the best way for you to keep in mind the four truths to remember in your darkest hour? Is there a place you can save the list and easily refer back to it?

As we wrap up this series, think back to some of the lessons that have stood out to you the most over the last seven weeks. Share your insights with the group.

PRAYER DIRECTION:

As you pray together as a group, ask God to show you any areas of your life where you still need to trust him. Then ask for the strength to give up control and give those areas over to God.

Praise God once again for what he did for you on the cross. Pray that God will help you keep the lessons from this study in your heart and mind so you can confidently share the Good News in the days to come.

HELP FOR HOSTS

CONGRATULATIONS! As the host of your small group, you have responded to the call to help shepherd Jesus' flock. Few other tasks in the family of God surpass the contribution you will be making. As you prepare to facilitate your group, whether it is one session or the entire series, here are a few thoughts to keep in mind.

Remember you are not alone. God knows everything about you, and he knew you would be asked to facilitate your group. Even though you may not feel ready, this is common for all good hosts. God promises, *"I will never leave you; I will never abandon you"* (Hebrews 13:5 GNT). Whether you are facilitating for one evening, several weeks, or a lifetime, you will be blessed as you serve.

1. **DON'T TRY TO DO IT ALONE.** Pray right now for God to help you build a healthy team. If you can enlist a co-host to help you shepherd the group, you will find your experience much richer. This is your chance to involve as many people as you can in building a healthy group. All you have to do is ask people to help. You'll be surprised at the response.

2. **BE FRIENDLY AND BE YOURSELF.** God wants to use your unique gifts and temperament. Be sure to greet people at the door with a big smile . . . this can set the mood for the whole gathering. Remember, they are taking as big a step to show up at your house as you are to host a small group! Don't try to do things exactly like another host; do them in a way that fits you. Admit when you don't have an answer and apologize when you make a mistake. Your group will love you for it and you'll sleep better at night.

3. **PREPARE FOR YOUR MEETING AHEAD OF TIME.** Review the session and write down your responses to each question. Pay special attention to the **Putting It Into Practice** exercises that ask group members to do something other than engage in discussion. These exercises will help your group live what the Bible teaches, not just talk about it.

4. **PRAY FOR YOUR GROUP MEMBERS BY NAME.** Before you begin your session, take a few moments and pray for each member by name. You may want to review the **Small Group Prayer and Praise Report** at least once a week. Ask God to use your time together to touch the heart of each person in your group. Expect God to lead you to whomever he wants you to encourage or challenge in a special way. If you listen, God will surely lead.

5. **WHEN YOU ASK A QUESTION, BE PATIENT.** Someone will eventually respond. Sometimes people need a moment or two of silence to think about the question. If silence doesn't bother you, it won't bother anyone else. After someone responds, affirm the response with a simple "thanks" or "great answer." Then ask, "How about somebody else?" or "Would someone who hasn't shared like to add anything?" Be sensitive to new people or reluctant members who aren't ready to say, pray, or do anything. If you give them a safe setting, they will blossom over time. If someone in your group is a wallflower who sits silently through every session, consider talking to them privately and encouraging them to participate. Let them know how important they are to you—that they are loved and appreciated, and that the group would value their input. Remember, still water often runs deep.

6. **PROVIDE TRANSITIONS BETWEEN QUESTIONS.** Ask if anyone would like to read the paragraph or Bible passage. Don't call on anyone, but ask for a volunteer, and then be patient until someone begins. Be sure to thank the person who reads aloud.

7. **BREAK INTO SMALLER GROUPS OCCASIONALLY.** With a greater opportunity to talk in a small circle, people will connect more with the study, apply more quickly what they're learning, and ultimately get more out of their small group experience. A small circle also encourages a quiet person to participate and tends to minimize the effects of a more vocal or dominant member.

8. **SMALL CIRCLES ARE ALSO HELPFUL DURING PRAYER TIME.** People who are unaccustomed to praying aloud will feel more comfortable trying it with just two or three others. Also, prayer requests won't take as much time, so circles will have more time to actually pray. When you gather back with the whole group, you can have one person from each circle briefly update everyone on the prayer requests from their subgroups. The other great aspect of subgrouping is that it fosters leadership development. As you ask people in the group to facilitate discussion or to lead a prayer circle, it gives them a small leadership step that can build their confidence.

9. **ROTATE FACILITATORS OCCASIONALLY.** You may be perfectly capable of hosting each time, but you will help others grow in their faith and gifts if you give them opportunities to host the group.

10. **ONE FINAL CHALLENGE (FOR NEW OR FIRST-TIME HOSTS).** Before your first opportunity to lead, look up each of the seven passages listed on page 72. Read each one as a devotional exercise to help prepare you with a shepherd's heart. Trust us on this one. If you do this, you will be more than ready for your first meeting.

FREQUENTLY ASKED QUESTIONS

HOW LONG WILL THIS GROUP MEET?

This study is seven sessions long. We encourage your group to add a session for a celebration. In your final session, each group member may decide if he or she desires to continue on for another study. At that time you may also want to do some informal evaluation, discuss your **Small Group Guidelines**, and decide which study you want to do next. We recommend you visit our website at pastors.com for more video-based small group studies.

WHO IS THE HOST?

The host is the person who coordinates and facilitates your group meetings. In addition to a host, we encourage you to select one or more group members to lead your group discussions. Several other responsibilities can be rotated, including serving refreshments, overseeing prayer requests, facilitating worship, or keeping up with those who miss a meeting. Shared ownership in the group helps everybody grow.

WHERE DO WE FIND NEW GROUP MEMBERS?

Recruiting new members can be a challenge for groups, especially new groups with just a few people, or existing groups that lose a few people along the way. We encourage you to use the Circles of Life diagram on page 66 of this study guide to brainstorm a list of people from your workplace, church, school, neighborhood, family, and so on. Then pray for the people on each member's list. Allow each member to invite several people from their list. Some groups fear that newcomers will interrupt the intimacy that members have built over time. However, groups that welcome newcomers generally gain strength with the infusion of new blood. Remember, the next person you add just might become a friend for eternity. Logistically, groups find different ways to add members. Some groups remain permanently open, while others choose to open periodically, such as at the beginning or end of a study. If your group becomes too large for easy, face-to-face conversations, you can subgroup, forming a second discussion group in another room.

HOW DO WE HANDLE CHILDCARE NEEDS?

Childcare needs must be handled very carefully. This is a sensitive issue. We suggest you seek creative solutions as a group. One common solution is to have the adults meet in the living room and share the cost of a babysitter (or two) who can be with the kids in another part of the house. Another popular option is to have one home for the kids and a second home (close by) for the adults. If desired, the adults could rotate the responsibility of providing a lesson for the kids. This last option is great with school-age kids and can be a huge blessing to families.

CIRCLES OF LIFE

Discover Who You Can Connect in Community. Use the chart on the following page to help carry out one of the values in the Small Group Guidelines, to "Welcome Newcomers."

FOLLOW THIS SIMPLE THREE-STEP PROCESS:

1. List one or two people in each circle.
2. Prayerfully select a person or couple from your list and tell your group about them.
3. Give them a call and invite them to your next meeting. Over 50 percent of those invited to a small group say, "Yes!"

FAMILY
(immediate or extended)

_____

_____

FELLOWSHIP
(church relationships)

_____

_____

FRIENDS
(neighbors, kids, sports, school, etc.)

_____

_____

FUN
(gym, hobbies, hangouts)

_____

_____

FACTORY/ FIRM
(work, professional arena)

_____

_____

SMALL GROUP GUIDELINES

It's a good idea for every group to put words to their shared values, expectations, and commitments. Such guidelines will help you avoid unspoken agendas and unmet expectations. We recommend you discuss your guidelines during Session 1 in order to lay the foundation for a healthy group experience. Feel free to modify anything that does not work for your group.

WE AGREE TO THE FOLLOWING VALUES:

CLEAR PURPOSE	To grow healthy spiritual lives by building a healthy small group community.
GROUP ATTENDANCE	To give priority to the group meeting (call if I am absent or late).
SAFE ENVIRONMENT	To create a safe place where people can be heard and feel loved (no quick answers, snap judgments, or simple fixes).
BE CONFIDENTIAL	To keep anything that is shared strictly confidential and within the group.
CONFLICT RESOLUTION	To avoid gossip and to immediately resolve any concerns by following the principles of Matthew 18:15-17.
SPIRITUAL HEALTH	To give group members permission to speak into my life and help me live a healthy, balanced spiritual life that is pleasing to God.
LIMIT OUR FREEDOM	To limit our freedom by not serving or consuming alcohol during small group meetings or events so as to avoid causing a weaker brother or sister to stumble (1 Corinthians 8:1-13; Romans 14:19-21).
WELCOME NEWCOMERS	To invite friends who might benefit from this study and warmly welcome newcomers.
BUILDING RELATIONSHIPS	To get to know the other members of the group and pray for them regularly.
OTHER	_____
	_____
	_____

CHILDCARE   _____

STARTING TIME   _____

ENDING TIME   _____

SMALL GROUP CALENDAR

Healthy groups share responsibilities and group ownership. It might take some time for this to develop. Shared ownership ensures that responsibility for the group doesn't fall to one person. Use the calendar to keep track of social events, mission projects, birthdays, or days off. Complete this calendar at your first or second meeting. Planning ahead will increase attendance and shared ownership.

DATE	LESSON	LOCATION	FACILITATOR	SNACK OR MEAL
	Session 1			
	Session 2			
	Session 3			
	Session 4			
	Session 5			
	Session 6			
	Session 7			
	Celebration			

SMALL GROUP PRAYER
AND PRAISE REPORT

This is a place where you can write each other's requests for prayer. You can also make a note when God answers a prayer. Pray for each other's requests. If you're new to group prayer, it's okay to pray silently or to pray by using just one sentence:

"God, please help _____ to _____ ."

DATE/PERSON	PRAYER REQUEST	PRAISE REPORT

ANSWER KEY

1.) We <u>BURY</u> it.
- <u>MINIMIZE</u>
- <u>RATIONALIZE</u>
- <u>COMPROMISE</u>

2.) We <u>BLAME</u> others.

3.) We <u>BEAT</u> ourselves up.

1.) <u>ADMIT</u> it.

To stop <u>DEFEATING</u> myself, I must stop <u>DECEIVING</u> myself.

2.) <u>ACCEPT</u> responsibility.

3.) <u>ASK</u> for forgiveness.

1.) God forgives <u>INSTANTLY</u>.

2.) God forgives <u>COMPLETELY</u>.

3.) God forgives <u>REPEATEDLY</u>.

4.) God forgives <u>FREELY</u>.

1.) I must know <u>I'LL FACE GOD</u> after I die.

2.) I must know that I've <u>SINNED AGAINST GOD</u>.

3.) I must know that Jesus was <u>MORE THAN A MAN</u>.

4.) I must know that only <u>GOD'S GRACE</u> can save me.

5.) I must know Jesus will save me <u>IF I ASK</u>.

On the <u>PROMISE</u> of God's Word

- <u>IMMEDIATE</u> ("Today")
- <u>CERTAIN</u> ("you will")
- <u>A RELATIONSHIP</u> ("be with me")
- <u>FOREVER</u> ("in paradise")

1.) Care for my <u>OWN FAMILY</u>.
- By <u>PAYING ATTENTION</u>
- By meeting <u>PRACTICAL NEEDS</u>
- By giving <u>EMOTIONAL SUPPORT</u>

2.) Treat <u>OTHER BELIEVERS</u> as my family.

3.) Learn to see <u>OTHERS' PAIN</u> even when I'm in pain.

4.) Meet <u>OTHERS' NEEDS</u> even if mine aren't met.

Look for Jesus disguised as a <u>HURTING PERSON</u>

- <u>REMEMBER</u> that Jesus cares about your pain.
- <u>ACCEPT</u> love from others.
- <u>LOOK FOR</u> somebody else to help.

Jesus became my <u>SUBSTITUTE</u>.

1.) God is <u>HOLY</u>!

2.) Sin is <u>UGLY</u>!

- Sin <u>ALIENATES</u> me from God

- Sin <u>DISTRESSES</u> me

- Sin <u>CONDEMNS</u> me

3.) Salvation is <u>COSTLY</u>.

1.) <u>TURN</u> from my sin and <u>TRUST</u> Jesus to save me.

2.) Live in a state of <u>GRATITUDE</u>.

3.) When I'm tempted, <u>REMEMBER</u> what my sin cost Jesus.

4.) Tell others <u>THE GOOD NEWS</u>!

1.) It showed that Jesus is <u>TRULY HUMAN</u>.

2.) It showed he was the <u>PROMISED SAVIOR</u>.

3.) It shows how much Jesus <u>LOVES ME</u>.

1.) I serve Jesus by <u>SERVING OTHERS</u>.

2.) Jesus notices the <u>SMALLEST SERVICE</u>.

3.) The most Christ-like service is to <u>ENEMIES</u>.

1.) Realize what I'm <u>REALLY THIRSTY FOR</u>.

2.) Realize that Jesus <u>FEELS MY PAIN</u>.

3.) Stop looking for <u>FULFILLMENT</u> elsewhere.

1.) He <u>FULFILLED</u> what God had promised us.

2.) He <u>SATISFIED</u> what God's justice required.

3.) He <u>PAID OFF</u> the debt that I owed God.

4.) He <u>DEFEATED</u> the fear of death!

5.) He <u>DESTROYED</u> Satan's power to <u>CONTROL</u> me.

- <u>VOLUNTARILY</u>

- <u>CONFIDENTLY</u>

- <u>TRUSTING GOD</u>

Jesus focused on the <u>FATHER</u>, not his pain.

1.) I have a Father in Heaven who <u>LOVES ME</u>!

2.) My Father can be <u>TRUSTED</u>!

3.) My Father is taking care of things <u>I CAN'T SEE</u>!

4.) My Father can handle anything I put <u>IN HIS HANDS</u>.

- Big enough to <u>BLESS ME</u>.

- Strong enough to keep me <u>ETERNALLY SECURE</u>.

- Scarred with the nail prints so he <u>CAN'T FORGET ME</u>.

KEY VERSES

"Jesus said, 'Father, forgive them,
for they do not know what they are doing.'"
LUKE 23:34 (NIV)

"And Jesus replied, 'I assure you,
today you will be with me in paradise.'"
LUKE 23:43 (NLT)

"When Jesus saw his mother standing there beside the disciple he loved,
he said to her, 'Dear woman, here is your son.' And he said to this
disciple, 'Here is your mother.'"
JOHN 19:26-27 (NLT)

"At noon, darkness fell across the whole land until three o'clock.
At about three o'clock, Jesus called out with a loud voice,
'Eli, Eli, lema sabachthani?' which means, 'My God, my God,
why have you abandoned me?'"
MATTHEW 27:45-46 (NLT)

"After this, Jesus knew that everything had been done. So that the
Scripture would come true, he said, 'I am thirsty.'"
JOHN 19:28 (NCV)

"When he had received the drink [of wine vinegar], *Jesus said,*
'It is finished.' With that, he bowed his head and gave up his spirit."
JOHN 19:30 (NIV)

"Then Jesus shouted, 'Father, I entrust my spirit into your hands!'
And with those words he breathed his last."
LUKE 23:46 (NLT)

NOTES & PRAYERS

NOTES & PRAYERS

....

....

....

....

....

....

....

....

....

....

....

....

....

....

....

....

....

....

....

....

....

....

....

....

....

....

....

....

....

....

....

....

....

....

....

....

....

NOTES & PRAYERS

....

....

....

....

....

....

....

....

....

....

....

....

....

....

....

....

....

....

....

....

....

....

....

....

....

....

....

....

....

....

....

....

....

....

....

....

....